Hi! I'm Nomi and this is my
stuffed bunny and best friend, Brave!

We have a great adventure
planned for us today.
Dinosaurs roamed the Earth many years ago,
and we get to see them!

Do you want to come with us?!

Let's GO!

Shhh be quiet. We must stay back.
This one is hungry and might need a snack.

Look at those TEETH in his great big head.
In one big gulp, he could swallow my bed!

Must be a Tyrannosaurus Rex

Now you would make the perfect pet!
I'll feed you grass and scratch your neck.

And on our walks, your great big SPIKES,
Will keep us safe from a T-rex bite!

Must be a Stegosaurus

Working together, they're smart and sneaky.
Look at those CLAWS! Do you feel uneasy?

Well this has been fun,
but it's time we run!
Let's back away,
before we're the prey.

Must be a Velociraptor

Fancy seeing you here! You like water too?!
We brought along our fishing pole. Can we fish with you?

With that big SAIL on your back, you can lead the way.
Take us to your favorite spot, just around the bay.

Must be a Spinosaurus

Look at those horns! 1, 2, 3!
Brave do you want to ride with me?

We rush through the forest, his feet shake the ground.
Brave, yee-hoo! Hold on to his CROWN!

Must be a Triceratops

Look at that ARMOR! You're ready for battle.
I like your big tail, it looks like my rattle!

Roaming around, eating every last veggie,
Never afraid, as you stand strong and mighty.

Must be an Anklyosaurus

Well you look sweet! Do you want a treat?
Come over here and have a leaf.

What a long NECK. It's not just for reaching!
Brave, climb on!
Are you thinking, what I'm thinking?...........

Must be a Brachiosaurus

I never knew dinosaurs could be so much fun.
What a great adventure! We're glad you could come.

You'll have to wait and see what adventure comes next!
But for now, it's nap time. Let's all get some rest.